FAF DU PLESSIS
COLOUR

SOUTH AFRICAN CRICKETER

MR VIVEK KUMAR PANDEY
SHAMBHUNATH

ISBN 979-888546349-2

Short biography of Faf du Plessis and about life.During writing this book no character & no religious are harmed written by Mr Vivek Kumar Pandey. winner youngest writer award 1st rank in india 2020.He is only one writer can publish 700+ own book that was greatest successfull in his life .This book fully colour edition books.

Contents

Foreword

Author biography in English :MY NAME IS VIVEK KUMAR PANDEY . I WAS BORN IN 30 SEP 2002,I AM FROM SURAT GUJARAT INDIA.MY DREAM WAS TO BE GOOD WRITERS ,MY FAMILY SUPPORTED ME TO SUCCESSFUL AND I CAN DO IT MY SELF.How do I write? That is a question, I believe, that cannot be honestly answered by me."CELEBRATING YOUNGEST WRITER AWARD WINNER IN GUJARAT 1ST RANK" MR PANDEY JI . I may think I did a good job writing something when in reality it could be horrible. The reader is the one who decides the quality of my writing. I do not find writing to be natural to me and therefore find it to be a real challenge. My trick as a challenged writer is to do the best I can and know that I am happy with the final outcome. It may take a while to do my best and there may be quite a few problems I run into along the way.

I am not a greedy person those who are thinking about me and my self I never tried it anyone people suffering from sadness ,I trying to get promoted people suffering from happiness and joy in your Life Time. Now in current situation in India and also world people are unemployed and have no many but our indian governor help to people to get free food from ration card , i also take part in leadership team ,i am Motivational speaker , Film script writer. There was my two dream firstly writer and secondly actor & also my own film is upcoming soon i done almost completely completed script for my film .I AM GOING TO SAY WORD OF HEART TOUCH OUT PLEASE READ IT" , firstly i thanks my father he supports me in this field they always getting inspired me by own his words and behavior ,they always said that he was a biggest person in the world in future and also they purchase fruit and chocolate for me in anytime & anyway , firstly my father buy him then call me Vivek you want a chocolate i will say yes papa but how many tell me ,papa: you tell me how much i buy him i told 1 or 2 chocolate but my father purchase whole the boxes of chocolate and they get suprised me. MY FATHER WAS BORN IN " 20 SEPTEMBER" 1971 IN INDIA.

1) MY FATHER FAVORITE CLOTHES IS KURTA PAIJMA AND ALSO STYLES SHOE

2) FAVORITE SINGER IS KISHORE DA

3) FAVORITE STATE GUJARAT AND KOLKATA , HIS VILLAGE IN BIHAR

4) FAVORITE COLOR BLACK AND WHITE

THEY ALSO LOVE cricket like IPL and one day t-20 .they also like watching a News daily and heard the song daily ,they also interested in tik tok video but in current time tik tok is banned in india but also few videos are in you tube. In lockdown time my family and me very enjoy day daily. my father play daily ludo with his sister and son, daughter.they always loved tea and coffee anytime call me "। विवेक थोडा़ चाय बनाओना विवेक तुम्हारे हाथ का चाय अच्छा लगता है". I make it tea for my father but some reason after the April to june they are suffering from fever and cough , weakness on 6 June 2020 my father death. they not told me say bye bye his life. After death of 6 June on 10 june my mom and dad anniversary.but my father is Best in the world they can do anything for me please take care of father and respect it of your parents.

CHAPTER ONE

Faf du Plessis Colour

- Faf du Plessis

1. During writing this book no character & no religious are harmed written by Mr Vivek Kumar Pandey.

Francois "Faf" du Plessis born 13 July 1984 is a South African international cricketer and former captain of the South Africa national cricket team.

du Plessis is a right-handed middle-order batsman and part-time leg spin bowler. He has played South African domestic cricket for Northerns and the Titans, as well as matches for Lancashire County Cricket Club, Chennai Super Kings and Rising Pune Supergiant in the Indian Premier League.

He made his ODI debut against India in January 2011 and scored an unbeaten 60 runs, and made his Test debut in November 2012, becoming the fourth South African to score a Test century on debut. After making his T20 debut in September 2012, he was subsequently also named T20 captain of South Africa for the following Twenty20 series against New Zealand and confirmed full-time skipper in February 2013.

du Plessis took over the Test captaincy in December 2016 and assumed full-time captaincy in all formats of the game in August 2017 after teammate and former captain AB de Villiers relinquished the two limited overs captaincies.In February 2021 he announced his retirement from Test cricket in order to focus on the 2021 and 2022 ICC Men's T20 World Cups.

- Domestic and T20 franchise career

Du Plessis was given a six-month contract with Lancashire County Cricket Club for the 2008 season as a Kolpak player after impressing the board with good performances in the local Nottinghamshire leagues for Mansfield Hosiery Mills and in the Lancashire League for Todmorden. Following his initial stint with the club, du Plessis signed a new three-year deal. Lancashire coach Mike Watkinson praised du Plessis' fielding, saying "if there's a better fielder in county cricket I've not seen him this season". In March 2010, it was announced that du Plessis would no longer be allowed to play for Lancashire as a Kolpak player after changes to the Kolpak rules. In 2011, he was signed by Chennai Super Kings to play in the Indian Premier League.

Along with Jonathan Vandiar, Dean Elgar, and Ethi Mbhalati, du Plessis was one of four uncapped players to be named in South Africa's 30-man preliminary squad for the 2011 World Cup. He was named one of the five South Africa Cricket Annual's Players Of The Year in 2011.

In October 2018, he was named in Paarl Rocks' squad for the first edition of the Mzansi Super League T20 tournament. He was the leading run-scorer for the team in the tournament, with 318 runs in nine matches.

In June 2019, he was selected to play for the Edmonton Royals franchise team in the 2019 Global T20 Canada tournament. In September 2019, he was named in the squad for the Paarl Rocks team for the 2019 Mzansi Super League tournament.In October 2020, he was drafted by the Colombo Kings for the inaugural edition of the Lanka Premier League. In the same month, he was picked by Peshawar Zalmi to feature in the delayed playoffs of the fifth season of the Pakistan Super League as a replacement for Kieron Pollard. He appeared only in one match as Zalmi were eliminated from the tournament in the first eliminator.

In February 2021, he was signed by the Quetta Gladiators for the 2021 Pakistan Super League but, in June 2021, he was ruled out of the rest of the tournament due a concussion sustained during a match after colliding with teammate Mohammad Hasnain.He captained the Saint Lucia Kings in the 2021 Caribbean Premier League, and the Bangla Tigers in the 2021 T10 League. In November 2021, he was selected to play for the Jaffna Kings following the players' draft for the 2021 Lanka Premier League.

• International career

• Early days

Du Plessis made his ODI debut on 18 January 2011 against India and made unbeaten 60 runs. He was chosen ahead of Albie Morkel for the 2011 World Cup on the Indian Sub-continent and later made his Test debut for South Africa against Australia at the Adelaide Oval in 2012 as the number 6 batsman, replacing the injured JP Duminy.

He scored 188 runs in the match and was selected as Man-of-the-match for his resilient performance that ultimately led to the match being drawn and the series being square before the third and final Test in which he scored 78 runs the 1st innings and the last man to be dismissed, taking the South African score to 388 in reply to Australia's 550. In the 2nd innings, he scored a match-saving 110 not out from 376 balls over 466 minutes.

In the next test at WACA Ground, he scored a resilient unbeaten 78 from 142 balls to take his team's score to 225 in the 1st innings, from 75/6 with able support from Robin Peterson (31 off 45), Vernon Philander (30 from 54) and last man Morne Morkel (17 from 15). South Africa won the 3-match Test Series against Australia 1–0. In December 2012, he was named captain of the South African T20 team for three matches against New Zealand.

In October 2013, he was fined 50% of his match fee after being found guilty of ball tampering in a Test match against Pakistan.

In December 2013, he scored a test match saving hundred with a score of 134 off 309 balls against India while chasing 458 to win in the 4th innings. The match ended in a draw with South Africa on 450/7, only 8 runs short from what would have been the highest successful run chase in test match history. Du Plessis made his maiden ODI hundred on 27 August 2014 against Australia after scoring 106 off 98 balls while chasing 327 runs to win. His partnership of 206 runs with AB de Villiers for the 3rd wicket is the highest for South Africa against Australia.He was also named in the T20I XI by Cricinfo for his performances in 2013.

His second Hundred came only 6 days later in his next ODI match on 2 September 2014. He scored 126 from 109 balls against the same opposition although South Africa lost by 62 runs. After making his maiden ODI hundred on 27 August 2014, and a consecutive ODI hundred on 2 September 2014, Du Plessis followed with a third consecutive ODI hundred, scoring 121 off 140 balls, this time against Zimbabwe on 4 September 2014. (South Africa were playing an ODI tri-series with Australia and Zimbabwe.)

On 6 September 2014 against Australia, Du Plessis fell only four runs short of becoming the first batsman in history to score 4 ODI hundreds in a row. (This would also have been a record for the most ODI hundreds by a batsman in any ICC ODI tournament) He initially looked on course to achieve his 4th ODI hundred until his batting partner AB de Villiers hit 2 sixes and a four in quick succession, which meant Du Plessis had to obtain all the remaining runs in the game single-handedly if he was to reach this milestone. Needing only 1 run to win the game with plenty of wickets and balls in hand, Du Plessis was on 96 and therefore had to hit a boundary (barring any extras) in order to reach 4 ODI hundreds in a row, but while attempting to hit a boundary he was caught off the bowling of Australia's spear-head Mitchell Johnson. South Africa still went on to win the ODI match against Australia comfortably by 6 wickets. This victory also secured South Africa as the winners of the ODI tri-series, and Du Plessis subsequently became Man of the Series.

On 17 December 2014, Du Plessis set the record for playing the most number of international cricket innings before scoring a duck (108) and also became the only batsman to play in over 100 international innings before first ever duck. On 27 December 2014, Du Plessis scored his second first innings century at the same ground: St. George's Oval. On 11 January 2015, du Plessis scored 119 in 56 balls against West Indies, becoming the first South African to score centuries in all forms of the game.

- Record breaking year

For the 2016–17 Australian tour of South Africa to play five ODIs, du Plessis was named captain after original skipper AB de Villiers ruled out due to a surgery. On 2 October, du Plessis scored his sixth century in the second game and became the second cricketer to score centuries in all international formats as captain, after Sri Lanka's Tillakaratne Dilshan. During that same match at Johannesburg, du Plessis become the first batsman to score centuries in all three formats of cricket at a single venue. Till April 2018, he has scored 17 international centuries (seven Test, nine ODI and one T20I) and is the first South African to score a century in all international formats).

Du Plessis is the first player to score a century in an innings of a day/night Test as captain. In the same game he set the record for declaration of the lowest ever total ever as an unbeaten captain, where he remained unbeaten on 118 in South Africa's first innings score of 259/9 dec.

On 12 December 2016, with AB de Villiers stepping down as Test Captain, du Plessis also inherited the role.

On 7 February 2017, du Plessis scored 185 runs in the fourth ODI against Sri Lanka, the second highest individual score by a South African, just three runs short of Gary Kirsten's 188*.

- Captaincy and beyond

On 24 August 2017, ODI captain De Villiers stepped down from captaincy and Du Plessis was named as the captain in all three formats. On the same day, he was named as the captain of World XI team for the three T20Is in Lahore, Pakistan.Pakistan won the series 2–1.Following the conclusion of the series, Faf du Plessis said how much it meant for the people of Pakistan and that it hopefully will bring cricket back to the country.

In March 2019, in the second ODI against Sri Lanka, Du Plessis scored his 5,000th run in ODI cricket. The following month, he was named as the captain of South Africa's squad for the 2019 Cricket World Cup. He finished the tournament as the leading run-scorer for South Africa, with 387 runs in nine matches.

In August 2019, he was named the Men's Cricketer of the Year at Cricket South Africa's annual award ceremony. In December 2020, in the first Test against Sri Lanka, du Plessis scored his 4,000th run and his tenth century in Test cricket. He ended with 199, becoming the 13th player to be dismissed on 199 in Tests, and also won the man of the match award.

On 17 February 2021, Du plessis announced his retirement from Tests after leading South Africa in 36 Test matches.

- Centuries

Faf du Plessis has scored centuries (100 or more runs in a single innings) on 10 occasions in Test, 12 occasions in One Day Internationals (ODIs) and once in Twenty20 Internationals (T20Is).

He scored his first century in November 2012 against Australia on his debut, in the second innings of test match, in which he scored unbeaten 110 runs. His highest Test score came in December 2020 against Sri Lanka when he scored 199 in Centurion.

It was over three years later in his 51st ODI that he made his first ODI century, scoring 106 against Australia in Harare. His highest ODI score of 185 runs came on 7 February 2017, against Sri Lanka in Cape Town.During the course of the innings, he set the record for the second highest ODI score after 188 of Gary Kirsten.

He scored his maiden T20I century against the West Indies in January 2015,becoming the first South African to score centuries in all three formats of the game.

• Ball tampering

Twice, du Plessis has been found guilty of ball tampering during his international career. The first time was during The Oval Test match in 2013 against Pakistan. In 2016, du Plessis was caught again ball tampering during the Hobart Test match against Australia.

The first incident against Pakistan involved du Plessis rubbing the ball against a zip on his trousers in order to change the nature of the ball. This was caught on video and du Plessis was subsequently found guilty. He was fined 50% of his match fee. The second incident against Australia involved du Plessis rubbing what looked like a "lolly" or mint, on the ball in order to make one side sticky. Du Plessis denied any wrongdoing and he pleaded not guilty to the charge. His teammate Hashim Amla defended him in a statement to the Australian media about the incident stating that the tampering claims were "a joke" and called them "ridiculous".

Regardless of the denials, du Plessis was found guilty of ball tampering on 21 November 2016. He was subsequently fined 100% of his match fee for the second Test against Australia and he was given three demerit points. Four demerit points within 24 months leads to a one Test or two limited-over games suspension. Du Plessis played the next test and scored a century. The following month he was made captain of the South African cricket team.

• Personal life

Du Plessis attended Afrikaanse Hoër Seunskool (Afrikaans High School for Boys, also known as Affies), a public school located in Pretoria. He attended alongside fellow Titans cricketers AB de Villiers, Heino Kuhn and Jacques Rudolph. He is also a graduate of the University of Pretoria. Du Plessis is a second cousin of Namibian rugby player Marcel du Plessis. His father Francois Du Plessis played rugby in the centre position for Northern Transvaal in the 1980s. Du Plessis was featured in the music video for the song "Maak Jou Drome Waar", a duet by AB de Villiers and Ampie du Preez.

He married his long-time girlfriend Imari Visser in November 2013 at Kleine Zalze. They have a daughter, born in 2017. His sister Rhemi is married to fellow South African international cricketer Hardus Viljoen in December 2019.

Du Plessis is a Christian. Du Plessis has said, "I know that my purpose is about more than the runs I score on the cricket field. I hope to be able to spend time with people to show them the love of Jesus and see His love shine through them as well."

On 17 July 2020, du Plessis released a statement via Instagram, showing support for the Black Lives Matter movement, following fellow Protea player Lungi Ngidi's request for Cricket South Africa to be vocal about the movement and to address racism in cricket. Du Plessis admitted that due to his ignorance, he silenced the struggles of others when he previously stated he does not see colour: "[I] acknowledge that South Africa is still hugely divided by racism and it is my personal responsibility to do my best to emphasise, hear the stories, learn and then be part of the solution with my thoughts, words and actions". He concluded his statement, saying "All lives don't matter UNTIL black lives matter. I'm speaking up now, because if I wait to be perfect, I never will. I want to leave a legacy of empathy. The work needs to continue for the change to come and whether we agree or disagree, conversation is the vehicle for change".

CHAPTER TWO

Currently Faf du Plessis Play With Csk

- Chennai Super Kings (CSK)
- Currently Faf du Plessis Play With Csk
- Chennai Super Kings in 2022

The Chennai Super Kings (CSK) are a franchise cricket team based in Chennai, Tamil Nadu. They play in the Indian Premier League (IPL). Founded in 2008, the team plays its home matches at the M. A. Chidambaram Stadium in Chennai. The team is owned by Chennai Super Kings Cricket Ltd and India Cements is the major stakeholder. The team served a two-year suspension from the IPL starting July 2015 due to the involvement of their owners in the 2013 IPL betting case,and won the title in its comeback season of 2018. The team is captained by Mahendra Singh Dhoni and coached by Stephen Fleming. They are the current defending champions, having won the 2021 IPL season.

The Super Kings have won the IPL title four times (in 2010, 2011, 2018, and 2021), and have the highest win percentage of matches among all teams in the IPL (59.83%).They hold the records of most appearances in the playoffs (eleven) and the Final (nine) of the IPL. In addition, they have also won the Champions League Twenty20 in 2010 and 2014. The brand value of the Super Kings in 2019 is estimated to be around 732 crore (roughly $104 million), making them one of the most valuable IPL franchises.

• History

In September 2007, the Board of Control for Cricket in India (BCCI) announced the establishment of the Indian Premier League, a Twenty20 competition to be started in 2008. In January 2008, the BCCI unveiled the owners of eight city-based franchises. The Chennai franchise was sold to the India Cements for $91 million, making it the fourth most expensive team in the league behind Mumbai, Bangalore and Hyderabad.India Cements acquired the rights to the franchise for 10 years. Former ICC Chairman N. Srinivasan was the de facto owner of the Chennai Super Kings, by means of his position as the vice-chairman and managing director of India Cements Ltd. The franchisee was transferred to a separate entity named Chennai Super Kings Cricket Ltd., after the Supreme Court of India struck down the controversial amendment to the BCCI constitution's clause 6.2.4 that allowed board officials to have a commercial interest in the IPL and the Champions League Twenty20 on 22 January 2015.

• 2008–2009: First seasons

Chennai Super Kings playing the Kolkata Knight Riders at the M. A. Chidambaram Stadium in the 2008 Indian Premier League.

During the first player auctions for the inaugural IPL season conducted in January 2008, the Chennai franchise bought a number of contemporary star cricketers such as Mahendra Singh Dhoni, Matthew Hayden, Stephen Fleming, Muttiah Muralitharan and Michael Hussey. Dhoni became the costliest player of the auction, as the Chennai franchise bought him for $1.5 million. The franchise ᶇamed Dhoni as the captain of the team and appointed Kepler Wessels as the head coach. They played their first game on 19 April 2008 against Kings XI Punjab at Mohali. The Super Kings won the game by 33 runs after posting 240/5 in 20 overs, which was the highest total of the tournament, a record surpassed by themselves in 2010. The Super Kings ended the league stage with eight wins from 14 games and finished third on the points table.They beat the Kings XI Punjab by 9 wickets in the semifinal. The Super Kings faced the Rajasthan Royals in the final of the IPL at Mumbai. Batting first, the Super Kings scored 163/5 in 20 overs and lost the game by 3 wickets off the final delivery of the match. They also earned a spot in the inaugural Champions League Twenty20 along with Rajasthan, but the tournament was canceled due to the 2008 Mumbai attacks and the Super Kings, along with Rajasthan, received $5 million each as compensation. Fleming, who had decided to retire from all forms of the game after the first season of the IPL, took over as the coach of the Super Kings team from Wessels for the next season which was to be held in South Africa.

For the 2009 season, the Super Kings bought English all-rounder Andrew Flintoff for $1.55 million at the auction making him the highest-paid IPL cricketer along with English teammate Kevin Pietersen who was bought for the same amount by Royal Challengers Bangalore.However, Flintoff played only 3 matches for them before suffering a knee injury that ruled him out of the season. The Super Kings were also without the services of Hussey who had decided to skip the IPL season to focus on The Ashes. The Super Kings finished with 17 points from 14 matches and earned a second place at the league table. However, at the semi-finals, their hopes of entering the final for a second time were crushed by the Royal Challengers who beat them by 6 wickets. The Super Kings opener Matthew Hayden, who scored 572 runs in 12 innings with 5 half-centuries at an average of 52 and strike-rate of 145, won the Orange Cap for the leading run-scorer of the season and was also adjudged Player of the Tournament.

- 2010: IPL and CLT20 double

In 2010, the Super Kings struggled in the first half of the regular season, winning only two matches out of seven. They won four of their next five games in the season mainly due to the efforts of Murali Vijay and Suresh Raina. After a defeat at home to the Delhi Daredevils, the Super Kings were left with a must-win match against Kings XI Punjab at Dharamshala. The Super Kings won the match by six wickets as they chased down the target of 193 with two balls to spare with skipper Dhoni scoring an unbeaten 54 from 29 balls.Thus, with seven wins from 14 matches, Chennai finished with the same number of points as three other teams with two semi-final spots at stake. Chennai got the third place as they had the better net run rate of the four teams which finished on 14 points.

In the semifinal, the Super Kings scored a modest 142/7 in 20 overs against the defending champions Deccan Chargers. But an inspired bowling spell from Doug Bollinger (4/13 in four overs) did the most damage as the Chargers were bowled out for 104. This gave the Super Kings a 38-run victory that took them to the final. The Super Kings faced the tournament favourites Mumbai Indians at their home ground in the final.Suresh Raina's 57 (35) helped the Super Kings recover from 68/3 after 12 overs to put up 168/5 at the end of their 20 overs. Then, their spin duo of Ravichandran Ashwin and Muralitharan conceded only 41 runs in the 8 overs bowled between them to help the Super Kings won the game by 22 runs and secure their first ever IPL title.With this, the Super Kings also qualified for the 2010 Champions League Twenty20 that was held in South Africa.

At the Champions League, the Super Kings were placed in Group A along with champions of Twenty20 competitions from Australia, South Africa, New Zealand and Sri Lanka. The Super Kings topped the Group table with three wins and a Super Over defeat to the Victorian Bushrangers. In the semi-final at Durban, the Super Kings comprehensively defeated IPL rivals Royal Challengers Bangalore by 52 runs. Raina won the Man of the Match for his unbeaten 94 off 48 balls.

The Super Kings played their first CLT20 final at Johannesburg where they beat the Chevrolet Warriors by 8 wickets, becoming the first IPL team to win the CLT20.Murali Vijay won not only the

Man of the Match in the final for his 58 but also the Golden Bat for scoring the most runs in the tournament and Ashwin, who was the leading wicket-taker, was adjudged the Player of the Series. At the end of the season, Matthew Hayden decided to retire from the IPL.

- 2011–2015: Success and suspension

1. Suresh Raina is the leading run-scorer for the Super Kings.

In 2011, as two new teams were added to the IPL, the IPL Governing Council declared that each franchise could retain a maximum of four players of their squad, only three of whom can be Indian players, and the rest of the international players would be put in the mega-auction. The Chennai franchise, keen to have the same set of core players, retained captain MS Dhoni, vice-captain Suresh Raina, Murali Vijay and all-rounder Albie Morkel for a total of $4.5 million.

The retention left them with the power of spending only $4.5 million at the mega-auction. At the auction, they bought back some of their star players of previous seasons such as Hussey, Ashwin, Bollinger and Subramaniam Badrinath. In the 2011 IPL, they lost three of their first five games which placed them at the bottom of the ten-team points table.But then, they went on to win seven of their next eight games to finish second and register a spot in the knockout stages. They faced the top-ranked team Royal Challengers Bangalore in the Qualifying final which they won by 6 wickets thanks to an unbeaten 73 from Suresh Raina.In the final, they faced the same opponents again, which was held at their home ground Chepauk. Vijay and Hussey put on a 133-run first-wicket partnership that helped the Super Kings to post a total of 205/5. Their bowlers, then, restricted Bangalore to only 147 to take the Super Kings to the second consecutive title in the IPL. Vijay was awarded Man of the Match for his match-winning innings of 95. CSK also won all their home games that season becoming the first team in IPL to achieve the feat. However at the Champions League later that year, they won only one out of their four group matches and finished at the bottom.

In 2012, the franchise signed up Indian all-rounder Ravindra Jadeja for $2 million at the players' auction. They got off to a rather slow start in the regular season, winning only five of their first 12 games which put them in doubt of qualifying for the Playoffs. Then they won three of their last four matches and qualified for the Playoffs with a better net run rate than the Royal Challengers who also finished with the same number of points.

In the Eliminator, they beat the Mumbai Indians by 38 runs before comprehensively beating the table-toppers Delhi Daredevils in the Qualifying final by 86 runs. Murali Vijay, who struck his second IPL hundred (113 off 58 balls), won the Man of the Match.At the final, the Super Kings were defeated by 5 wickets by the Kolkata Knight Riders who chased down the target of 191 with two balls to spare, thus denying the Super Kings a hat-trick of titles in the IPL. At the Champions League, once again they could not progress past the group stage with two wins and two defeats.

In 2013, the Super Kings strengthened their bowling attack by signing up five overseas and five Indian bowlers. In the IPL season, they finished first in the points table with 11 wins from 16 matches and qualified for the Playoffs and 2013 CLT20.

This was the first time in six seasons that the Super Kings had topped the league table of the IPL. During the season, they also equaled Royal Challengers Bangalore's 2011 record for most wins in succession in the IPL (7 wins on trot).

In the first Qualifier at Delhi against Mumbai Indians, the Super Kings posted 192/1 in 20 overs riding on unbeaten half-centuries from Hussey (86* off 58 balls) and Raina (82* off 42 balls) before bowling out their opponents for 144. Thus they entered the final of the IPL for the fourth time in succession where they would play the same opponents, Mumbai Indians, at Kolkata. At the final, batting first, the Mumbai Indians made 148/9 in their 20 overs. In reply, the Super Kings were reduced to 39/6 at one stage before an unbeaten half-century from skipper Dhoni took them close to the target. However, Mumbai Indians won the match by 23 runs to win their first ever IPL title. Super Kings opening batsman Michael Hussey, who scored 733 runs that season at an average of 52, won the Orange Cap for the most runs in the season while all-rounder Dwayne Bravo won the Purple Cap for bagging the most wickets (32).

The Super Kings gained direct qualification for the 2013 CLT20 which was held in India in September–October. They were placed in Group B alongside Brisbane Heat, Sunrisers Hyderabad, Titans and Trinidad & Tobago. They won their first three games before losing the final group match against Trinidad & Tobago. With 12 points from four matches, the Super Kings progressed to the semifinals where they suffered a 14-run defeat at the hands of the Rajasthan Royals at Jaipur.

In 2014, before the players' mega-auction, Chennai retained Dhoni, Raina, Jadeja, Ashwin and Bravo. The retention left them with a purse of 21 crores to spend at the auction. At the auction, the franchise bought the likes of Brendon McCullum, Dwayne Smith, Faf du Plessis, Ashish Nehra, Mohit Sharma among others. The first phase of the IPL season, as it coincided with the general elections, was held in UAE. The second phase returned to India, but the Super Kings' home matches were shifted from Chennai, due to "a deadlock between stadium authorities and the state administration", to JSCA International Stadium in Ranchi. The Super Kings started the season with a defeat in the opening match, after which they went on to win eight of their next nine matches to take the first spot in the points table.

However, they suffered a loss of form towards the end of the regular season which resulted in three consecutive defeats. They won their last league fixture and finished third in the points table and qualified for the Eliminator against the fourth-placed Mumbai Indians. They won the Eliminator at Mumbai by 7 wickets and qualified for the Qualifier. At the Qualifier against Kings XI Punjab, the Super Kings won the toss and elected to field. Punjab went on to score 226/6 in their 20 overs. The Super Kings, in reply, could manage only 202/7 despite a 25-ball 87 from Raina.

They crashed out of the IPL, but, on account of finishing third, qualified for the main event of the 2014 CLT20. In the group stage of the CLT20, the Super Kings won two matches, lost one while another match was a no result. Thus with 10 points they finished second in the group table and qualified for the semifinal where they met the unbeaten team of the other group, Kings XI Punjab. After being put in to bat, the Super Kings posted 182/7 in 20 overs thanks to Bravo who scored a 39-ball 67. Then their bowlers reduced Punjab to 34/6 in the eighth over, before eventually bowling them out for 117. At the final in Bangalore, the Super Kings faced the IPL champions Kolkata Knight Riders who set them a target of 181 in 20 overs. Raina guided the run-chase with an unbeaten 109 off 62 balls, helping the team to an eight-wicket win and their second CLT20 title. Super Kings spinner Pawan Negi who took 5/22 during Kolkata's innings won the Man of the Match, and Raina, who finished as the highest run-getter of the tournament, was awarded Man of the Tournament.

In 2015, before the players' auction, Chennai Super Kings gave away Ben Hilfenhaus, John Hastings, Vijay Shankar and David Hussey. At the auction they bought back Michael Hussey for a price of 1.5 crores. They also bought Kyle Abbott, Irfan Pathan, Andrew Tye, Eklavya Dwivedi, Ankush Bains, Pratyush Singh and Rahul Sharma. In the final, they lost against Mumbai.

• 2018–present

Chennai Super Kings playing the Kings XI Punjab in the 2018 Indian Premier League at the MCA Stadium in Pune, Maharashtra.

• 2018

Ahead of the players mega auction, Chennai Super Kings retained Mahendra Singh Dhoni, Suresh Raina & Ravindra Jadeja. Additionally, Faf du Plessis and Dwayne Bravo were brought back into the side using RTM. The return of the Super Kings to the IPL was the cause of a large amount of celebration and fanfare amongst the fans, with a crowd of more than 10,000 turning up for the practice sessions held at the M. A. Chidambaram Stadium in Chennai before the start of the tournament.

Chennai's campaign started off with a thrilling one wicket win over the Mumbai Indians in the first match of the season thanks to an unbeaten 68 off 30 balls from Dwayne Bravo. Playing their first home game in Chennai, the Kings successfully managed to chase down a target of 202 set by the Kolkata Knight Riders, aided by a quickfire half-century by Sam Billings. The team then went on to lose to Kings XI Punjab in Mohali but bounced back by winning three matches in a row against the Rajasthan Royals, Sunrisers Hyderabad and Royal Challengers Bangalore. The Super Kings' next eight matches resulted in them alternating between victories and defeats by winning against the Delhi Daredevils, Royal Challengers Bangalore, Sunrisers Hyderabad and Kings XI Punjab and losing against the Mumbai Indians, Rajasthan Royals, Delhi Daredevils and the Kolkata Knight Riders. The league stage ended with the Super Kings in second place behind the Sunrisers.Chennai then went on to post back-to-back victories against the Sunrisers Hyderabad in the first qualifier and in the final to win the Indian Premier League for the third time since the inception of the tournament. Star all-rounder Shane Watson was ajudged Man of the Match for his 117* from 57 balls.

Three of the five centuries scored in the 2018 season were by players belonging to the Chennai Super Kings (Ambati Rayudu 100* and Shane Watson 106, 117*). The Super Kings also became the first team to defeat an opposing team (Sunrisers Hyderabad) four times in a single season.

• 2019

In 2019, the Super Kings was the first team to qualify for the Playoffs. They entered the final of the IPL for the eighth time in the league. At the final, batting first, the Mumbai Indians made 149/8 in their 20 overs. In reply, the Super Kings were able to make just one short of Mumbai's total 148/7 and lost the title. Super Kings' star bowler of the season Imran Tahir, who took 26 wickets, won the Purple Cap for bagging the most wickets.

- 2020

Before the 2020 season of the IPL, CSK roped in Sam Curran (5.5 crore), Josh Hazlewood (2 crore), Piyush Chawla (6.75 crore) and R. Sai Kishore (20 lakh). But due to the COVID-19 pandemic, the IPL was postponed and shifted to the UAE. CSK faced some early setbacks before the start of the season after cricketers Ruturaj Gaikwad and Deepak Chahar tested positive for the coronavirus. CSK's star batsman and vice-captain Suresh Raina and spinner Harbhajan Singh pulled out of the IPL citing personal reasons.

Despite the setbacks, CSK started the season off on a high by convincingly beating the defending champions Mumbai Indians in the inaugural game.But it was all downhill from here. CSK lost their next three games to the Rajasthan Royals, Delhi Capitals and the Sunrisers Hyderabad. This was followed by an out of the blue 10 wicket win over the Kings XI Punjab. The team then lost their next two matches to the Kolkata Knight Riders and the Royal Challengers Bangalore. CSK captain MS Dhoni drew a lot of criticism from the fans and supporters over his form and team selection after his comments on the team youngsters lacking the "spark" to be backed by the management.

1. CSK were at the bottom of the table for most of the season and their play-offs hopes were crushed after facing a humiliating 10 wickets defeat against the Mumbai Indians.
2. CSK ended their campaign on a high note by winning their last three games against KKR, RCB and KXIP, thanks to a hat-trick of fifties by youngster Ruturaj Gaikwad. He also became the first ever CSK cricketer to score three consecutive fifties in the

team's history. CSK finished 7th overall in the points table and failed to make the playoffs for the very first time.

3. CSK released many of their bad performers from the previous season like Piyush Chawla, Kedar Jadhav and Murali Vijay before the player auctions for the 2021 season of the IPL.

- 2021

During the 2021 auctions, CSK picked up Test specialist Cheteshwar Pujara for base price of Rs 50 lakh while spending a whopping Rs 9.25 crore on Krishnappa Gowtham, making the spinner the most expensive uncapped Indian buy ever. They also bought English all-rounder Moeen Ali for Rs 7 crore. Along with the three, CSK brought some uncapped Indian talents like Harishankar Reddy, Bhagath Varma and Chezhian Harinishanth for their base price of Rs 20 lakh each. Rajasthan Royals player Robin Uthappa was traded to the Super Kings as well.

CSK begun the first leg of the 2021 season with a loss against Delhi capitals. After that, they carried a consecutive 5 match winning streak, followed by a defeat against Mumbai Indians. Following the second wave of the COVID-19 pandemic, and the rise in COVID-19 positive cases in many team camps, the IPL was postponed.

When the second leg of the IPL resumed in the UAE, CSK carried a consecutive 4 match winning streak and thus, ensured its berth in the playoffs. CSK was the first team to qualify for playoffs in the 2021 season. CSK completed the league stage by losing the last 3 matches. Yet, CSK managed to remain within top 2 places in the points table throughout the season.

In Qualifier 1, CSK beat Delhi Capitals to storm into finals for the 9th time in their history. In the finals, CSK showcased an all-round performance against KKR to clinch their 4th IPL title.

- Home ground

The home ground of the Super Kings is the historic M. A. Chidambaram Stadium (commonly called "The Chepauk") located in Chennai. The stadium is named after former BCCI President M. A. Chidambaram. It is the oldest stadium in India which is in continuous use. The stadium is owned by the Tamil Nadu Cricket Association and has a seating capacity of 50,000 as of May 2013. In 2010, the stadium underwent a major renovation for hosting some of the matches of the 2011 ICC Cricket World Cup. The seating capacity was increased from 36,000 to 50,000 and three new stands were established during this renovation.

The Super Kings have a 67.44% win record at this venue, which is often referred to as "Fortress Chepauk"and "Lions' den". In the 2011 season, the Super Kings won all their home games (8 matches) including the final against Royal Challengers Bangalore. The Super Kings thus became the first team to win all their home games in a season and also the first team to win the tournament at home.

In 2014, Chennai Super Kings played all their home matches at Ranchi due to issues with Government of Tamil Nadu.

In 2018, Chennai Super Kings managed to play a solitary home game against Kolkata Knight Riders due to members of a few fringe political parties staging protests outside the stadium as well as several parts of Chennai, demanding the IPL matches to be moved out of the city until the Cauvery Management Board (CMB) was set up as directed by the honourable Supreme Court of India. Despite tight security for the match against KKR, the Chennai police expressed their inability in ensuring enough personnel at the venue for the smooth conduct of the remaining games. The remaining six home matches of Chennai Super Kings were moved out of Chennai. Maharashtra Cricket Association Stadium in Pune was selected to host the remaining six home matches of Chennai Super Kings.

• Mahendra Singh Dhoni is the first Indian captain to win the IPL.

Mahendra Singh Dhoni, who was the captain of the Indian limited-overs team in 2008, was bought by the Super Kings for $1.5

million at the 2008 players' auction. He was the most expensive player in the IPL until 2009 when the Super Kings signed up English all-rounder Andrew Flintoff for $1.55 million. Dhoni is one of the most successful captains in the IPL, having led the Super Kings to nine finals of which the team has won four.

The vice-captain of the team from 2008 to 2015 was Suresh Raina. Raina holds multiple IPL records such as most caps, most runs and most catches.Australian batsman Michael Hussey has the best batting average for the Super Kings.He was the first batsman from the Super Kings to score a century in the IPL. After Matthew Hayden's retirement in 2010, Hussey took over his place of opening batsman and was the team's leading run-scorer in 2011 and 2013 seasons. Murali Vijay, who played for the team from 2009 to 2013, is the first Indian batsman to score two centuries in the IPL. Super Kings' spinner Ravichandran Ashwin has the third best economy rate in IPL (6.53)and is the leading wicket-taker for the team.

• Identity

Some of this section's listed sources may not be reliable. Please help this article by looking for better, more reliable sources. Unreliable citations may be challenged or deleted. (April 2018)

• Name, logo, crest and colors

The Chennai franchise named the team as Chennai Super Kings to honour the rulers of the Tamil empire. The word "super" is used commonly in southern India especially in Tamil Nadu. The team name also derives from India Cements' brand "Coromandel King".

The team logo features the head of a roaring lion in orange and the team name rendered in blue. The crown above the team name is the same as that used in the logo of the brand Coromandel King. According to the logo designers, since the lion is the king of the jungle, the roaring lion logo reflects the team name. The details of the logo signifies various qualities such as youth, vibrancy, solid performance orientation and fiery spirit.

The team's primary colour is yellow with blue and orange stripes on either sides of the jersey. The jersey also incorporates the roaring lion logo in the center of the shirt below the logo of the main sponsor. The basic look of the jersey has remained the same from the first season with no changes except for the sponsor placement. The kit manufacturer until 2014 was Reebok and from 2015, Australian Apparel and Sports Gear manufacturer Spartan manufactures kits for the team.

• Theme song

The team's theme song is the "Whistle Podu" designed by Aravind–Shankar (duo of Aravind Murali and Jaishankar Iyer). Although the track was created only for YouTube in 2008, it gained popularity during the 2009 season and later became the team's theme song. The video of the song represents the street dance form of dappangutthu which is very popular among certain communities in Tamil Nadu. It is also a folk dance and music genre employed in Tamil cinema. The recordings of some of the Super Kings players whistling were used in the music video.

• Kit and sponsors

Myntra signed a deal for principal shirt sponsor for the 2021 Season. Muthoot Group was one of the principal shirt sponsors, having signed a three-year deal in 2018.Telecom service provider Aircel was the previous shirt sponsor after they signed a three-year deal in 2008 which was then renewed in 2011 for 850 million, then the most expensive sponsorship deal in IPL. The team also has sponsorship deals with India Cements, Gulf Oil, Equitas Small Finance Bank, HIL, Nippon Paint, Parle Agro Frooti and Atria Convergence Technologies.

CHAPTER THREE

Let's Know About Cricket

- Cricket

Cricket is a bat-and-ball game played between two teams of eleven players on a field at the centre of which is a 22-yard (20-metre) pitch with a wicket at each end, each comprising two bails balanced on three stumps. The game proceeds when a player on the fielding team, called the bowler, "bowls" (propels) the ball from one end of the pitch towards the wicket at the other end. The batting side's players score runs by striking the bowled ball with a bat and running between the wickets, while the bowling side tries to prevent this by keeping the ball within the field and getting it to either wicket, and dismiss each batter (so they are "out"). Means of dismissal include being bowled, when the ball hits the stumps and dislodges the bails, and by the fielding side either catching a hit ball before it touches the ground, or hitting a wicket with the ball before a batter can cross the crease line in front of the wicket to complete a run. When ten batters have been dismissed, the innings ends and the teams swap roles. The game is adjudicated by two umpires, aided by a third umpire and match referee in international matches.

Forms of cricket range from Twenty20, with each team batting for a single innings of 20 overs and the game generally lasting three hours, to Test matches played over five days. Traditionally cricketers play in all-white kit, but in limited overs cricket they wear club or team colours. In addition to the basic kit, some players wear protective gear to prevent injury caused by the ball, which is a hard, solid spheroid made of compressed leather with a slightly raised sewn seam enclosing a cork core layered with tightly wound string.

The earliest reference to cricket is in South East England in the mid-16th century. It spread globally with the expansion of the British Empire, with the first international matches in the second half of the 19th century. The game's governing body is the International Cricket Council (ICC), which has over 100 members, twelve of which are full members who play Test matches. The game's rules, the Laws of Cricket, are maintained by Marylebone Cricket Club (MCC) in London. The sport is followed primarily in South Asia, Australasia, the United Kingdom, southern Africa and the West Indies.Women's cricket, which is organised and played separately, has also achieved international standard. The most successful side playing international cricket is Australia, which has won seven One Day International trophies, including five World Cups, more than any other country and has been the top-rated Test side more than any other country.

- History of cricket to 1725

A medieval "club ball" game involving an underhand bowl towards a batter. Ball catchers are shown positioning themselves to catch a ball. Detail from the Canticles of Holy Mary, 13th century.

Cricket is one of many games in the "club ball" sphere that basically involve hitting a ball with a hand-held implement; others include baseball (which shares many similarities with cricket, both belonging in the more specific bat-and-ball games category), golf, hockey, tennis, squash, badminton and table tennis. In cricket's case, a key difference is the existence of a solid target structure, the wicket (originally, it is thought, a "wicket gate" through which sheep were herded), that the batter must defend. The cricket historian Harry Altham identified three "groups" of "club ball" games: the "hockey group", in which the ball is driven to and fro between two targets (the goals); the "golf group", in which the ball is driven towards an undefended target (the hole); and the "cricket group", in which "the ball is aimed at a mark (the wicket) and driven away from it".

It is generally believed that cricket originated as a children's game in the south-eastern counties of England, sometime during the medieval period.Although there are claims for prior dates, the earliest definite reference to cricket being played comes from evidence given at a court case in Guildford in January 1597 (Old Style), equating to January 1598 in the modern calendar. The case concerned ownership of a certain plot of land and the court heard the testimony of a 59-year-old coroner, John Derrick, who gave witness that.

Being a scholler in the ffree schoole of Guldeford hee and diverse of his fellows did runne and play there at creckett and other plaies.

Given Derrick's age, it was about half a century earlier when he was at school and so it is certain that cricket was being played c. 1550 by boys in Surrey. The view that it was originally a children's game is reinforced by Randle Cotgrave's 1611 English-French dictionary in which he defined the noun "crosse" as "the crooked staff wherewith boys play at cricket" and the verb form "crosser" as "to play at cricket".

One possible source for the sport's name is the Old English word "cryce" (or "cricc") meaning a crutch or staff. In Samuel Johnson's Dictionary, he derived cricket from "cryce, Saxon, a stick". In Old French, the word "criquet" seems to have meant a kind of club or stick. Given the strong medieval trade connections between south-east England and the County of Flanders when the latter belonged to the Duchy of Burgundy, the name may have been derived from the Middle Dutch (in use in Flanders at the time) "krick"(-e), meaning a stick (crook). Another possible source is the Middle Dutch word "krickstoel", meaning a long low stool used for kneeling in church and which resembled the long low wicket with two stumps used in early cricket. According to Heiner Gillmeister, a European language expert of Bonn University, "cricket" derives from the Middle Dutch phrase for hockey, met de (krik ket)sen (i.e., "with the stick chase"). Gillmeister has suggested that not only the name but also the sport itself may be of Flemish origin.

- Growth of amateur and professional cricket in England

Evolution of the cricket bat. The original "hockey stick" (left) evolved into the straight bat from c. 1760 when pitched delivery bowling began.

Although the main object of the game has always been to score the most runs, the early form of cricket differed from the modern game in certain key technical aspects; the North American variant of cricket known as wicket retained many of these aspects. The ball was bowled underarm by the bowler and along the ground towards a batter armed with a bat that in shape resembled a hockey stick; the batter defended a low, two-stump wicket; and runs were called notches because the scorers recorded them by notching tally sticks.

In 1611, the year Cotgrave's dictionary was published, ecclesiastical court records at Sidlesham in Sussex state that two parishioners, Bartholomew Wyatt and Richard Latter, failed to attend church on Easter Sunday because they were playing cricket. They were fined 12d each and ordered to do penance.This is the earliest mention of adult participation in cricket and it was around the same time that the earliest known organised inter-parish or village match was played – at Chevening, Kent. In 1624, a player called Jasper Vinall died after he was accidentally struck on the head during a match between two parish teams in Sussex.

Cricket remained a low-key local pursuit for much of the 17th century. It is known, through numerous references found in the records of ecclesiastical court cases, to have been proscribed at times by the Puritans before and during the Commonwealth. The problem was nearly always the issue of Sunday play as the Puritans considered cricket to be "profane" if played on the Sabbath, especially if large crowds or gambling were involved.

According to the social historian Derek Birley, there was a "great upsurge of sport after the Restoration" in 1660. Gambling on sport became a problem significant enough for Parliament to pass the 1664 Gambling Act, limiting stakes to £100 which was, in any case, a colossal sum exceeding the annual income of 99% of the population. Along with prizefighting, horse racing and blood sports, cricket was perceived to be a gambling sport.Rich patrons made matches for high stakes, forming teams in which they engaged the first professional players.By the end of the century, cricket had developed into a major sport that was spreading throughout England and was already being taken abroad by English mariners and colonisers – the earliest reference to cricket overseas is dated 1676. A 1697 newspaper report survives of "a great cricket match" played in Sussex "for fifty guineas apiece" – this is the earliest known contest that is generally considered a First Class match.

- The patrons, and other players from the social class known as the "gentry", began to classify themselves as "amateurs" to establish a clear distinction from the professionals, who were invariably members of the working class, even to the point of having separate changing and dining facilities. The gentry, including such high-ranking nobles as the Dukes of Richmond, exerted their honour code of noblesse oblige to claim rights of leadership in any sporting contests they took part in, especially as it was necessary for them to play alongside their "social inferiors" if they were to win their bets. In time, a perception took hold that the typical amateur who played in first-class cricket, until 1962 when amateurism was abolished, was someone with a public school education who had then gone to one of Cambridge or Oxford University – society insisted that such people were "officers and gentlemen" whose destiny was to provide leadership. In a purely financial sense, the cricketing amateur would theoretically claim expenses for playing while his professional counterpart played under contract and was paid a wage or match fee; in practice, many amateurs claimed more than actual expenditure and the derisive term "shamateur" was coined to describe the practice.

• The Young Cricketer, 1768

The game underwent major development in the 18th century to become England's national sport.Its success was underwritten by the twin necessities of patronage and betting. Cricket was prominent in London as early as 1707 and, in the middle years of the century, large crowds flocked to matches on the Artillery Ground in Finsbury. The single wicket form of the sport attracted huge crowds and wagers to match, its popularity peaking in the 1748 season. Bowling underwent an evolution around 1760 when bowlers began to pitch the ball instead of rolling or skimming it towards the batter. This caused a revolution in bat design because, to deal with the bouncing ball, it was necessary to introduce the modern straight bat in place of the old "hockey stick" shape.

The Hambledon Club was founded in the 1760s and, for the next twenty years until the formation of Marylebone Cricket Club (MCC) and the opening of Lord's Old Ground in 1787, Hambledon was both the game's greatest club and its focal point. MCC quickly became the sport's premier club and the custodian of the Laws of Cricket. New Laws introduced in the latter part of the 18th century included the three stump wicket and leg before wicket (lbw).

The 19th century saw underarm bowling superseded by first roundarm and then overarm bowling. Both developments were controversial.Organisation of the game at county level led to the creation of the county clubs, starting with Sussex in 1839. In December 1889, the eight leading county clubs formed the official County Championship, which began in 1890.

The most famous player of the 19th century was W. G. Grace, who started his long and influential career in 1865. It was especially during the career of Grace that the distinction between amateurs and professionals became blurred by the existence of players like him who were nominally amateur but, in terms of their financial gain, de facto professional. Grace himself was said to have been paid more money for playing cricket than any professional.

The last two decades before the First World War have been called the "Golden Age of cricket". It is a nostalgic name prompted by the collective sense of loss resulting from the war, but the period did produce some great players and memorable matches, especially as organised competition at county and Test level developed.

- Cricket becomes an international sport

In 1844, the first-ever international match took place between the United States and Canada. In 1859, a team of English players went to North America on the first overseas tour. Meanwhile, the British Empire had been instrumental in spreading the game overseas and by the middle of the 19th century it had become well established in Australia, the Caribbean, India, Pakistan, New Zealand, North America and South Africa.

In 1862, an English team made the first tour of Australia. The first Australian team to travel overseas consisted of Aboriginal stockmen who toured England in 1868. The first One Day International match was played on 5 January 1971 between Australia and England at the Melbourne Cricket Ground.

In 1876–77, an England team took part in what was retrospectively recognised as the first-ever Test match at the Melbourne Cricket Ground against Australia. The rivalry between England and Australia gave birth to The Ashes in 1882, and this has remained Test cricket's most famous contest. Test cricket began to expand in 1888–89 when South Africa played England.

- World cricket in the 20th century

The inter-war years were dominated by Australia's Don Bradman, statistically the greatest Test batter of all time. Test cricket continued to expand during the 20th century with the addition of the West Indies (1928), New Zealand (1930) and India (1932) before the Second World War and then Pakistan (1952), Sri Lanka (1982), Zimbabwe (1992), Bangladesh (2000), Ireland and Afghanistan (both 2018) in the post-war period. South Africa was banned from international cricket from 1970 to 1992 as part of the apartheid boycott.

- The rise of limited overs cricket

Cricket entered a new era in 1963 when English counties introduced the limited overs variant. As it was sure to produce a result, limited overs cricket was lucrative and the number of matches increased. The first Limited Overs International was played in 1971 and the governing International Cricket Council (ICC), seeing its potential, staged the first limited overs Cricket World Cup in 1975. In the 21st century, a new limited overs form, Twenty20, made an immediate impact. On 22 June 2017, Afghanistan and Ireland became the 11th and 12th ICC full members, enabling them to play Test cricket.

- A typical cricket field.

In cricket, the rules of the game are specified in a code called The Laws of Cricket (hereinafter called "the Laws") which has a global remit. There are 42 Laws (always written with a capital "L"). The earliest known version of the code was drafted in 1744 and, since 1788, it has been owned and maintained by its custodian, the Marylebone Cricket Club (MCC) in London.

- Playing area

Cricket is a bat-and-ball game played on a cricket field between two teams of eleven players each. The field is usually circular or oval in shape and the edge of the playing area is marked by a boundary, which may be a fence, part of the stands, a rope, a painted line or a combination of these; the boundary must if possible be marked along its entire length.

In the approximate centre of the field is a rectangular pitch (see image, below) on which a wooden target called a wicket is sited at each end; the wickets are placed 22 yards (20 m) apart. The pitch is a flat surface 10 feet (3.0 m) wide, with very short grass that tends to be worn away as the game progresses (cricket can also be played on artificial surfaces, notably matting). Each wicket is made of three wooden stumps topped by two bails.

• Cricket pitch and creases

As illustrated above, the pitch is marked at each end with four white painted lines: a bowling crease, a popping crease and two return creases. The three stumps are aligned centrally on the bowling crease, which is eight feet eight inches long. The popping crease is drawn four feet in front of the bowling crease and parallel to it; although it is drawn as a twelve-foot line (six feet either side of the wicket), it is, in fact, unlimited in length. The return creases are drawn at right angles to the popping crease so that they intersect the ends of the bowling crease; each return crease is drawn as an eight-foot line, so that it extends four feet behind the bowling crease, but is also, in fact, unlimited in length.

Before a match begins, the team captains (who are also players) toss a coin to decide which team will bat first and so take the first innings. Innings is the term used for each phase of play in the match.In each innings, one team bats, attempting to score runs, while the other team bowls and fields the ball, attempting to restrict the scoring and dismiss the batters. When the first innings ends, the teams change roles; there can be two to four innings depending upon the type of match. A match with four scheduled innings is played over three to five days; a match with two scheduled innings is usually completed in a single day. During an innings, all eleven members of the fielding team take the field, but usually only two members of the batting team are on the field at any given time.

The exception to this is if a batter has any type of illness or injury restricting his or her ability to run, in this case the batter is allowed a runner who can run between the wickets when the batter hits a scoring run or runs,though this does not apply in international cricket. The order of batters is usually announced just before the match, but it can be varied.

The main objective of each team is to score more runs than their opponents but, in some forms of cricket, it is also necessary to dismiss all of the opposition batters in their final innings in order to win the match, which would otherwise be drawn. If the team batting last is all out having scored fewer runs than their opponents, they are said to have "lost by n runs" (where n is the difference between the aggregate number of runs scored by the teams). If the team that bats last scores enough runs to win, it is said to have "won by n wickets", where n is the number of wickets left to fall. For example, a team that passes its opponents' total having lost six wickets (i.e., six of their batters have been dismissed) have won the match "by four wickets".

In a two-innings-a-side match, one team's combined first and second innings total may be less than the other side's first innings total. The team with the greater score is then said to have "won by an innings and n runs", and does not need to bat again: n is the difference between the two teams' aggregate scores. If the team batting last is all out, and both sides have scored the same number of runs, then the match is a tie; this result is quite rare in matches of two innings a side with only 62 happening in first-class matches from the earliest known instance in 1741 until January 2017. In the traditional form of the game, if the time allotted for the match expires before either side can win, then the game is declared a draw.

If the match has only a single innings per side, then a maximum number of overs applies to each innings. Such a match is called a "limited overs" or "one-day" match, and the side scoring more runs wins regardless of the number of wickets lost, so that a draw cannot occur. In some cases, ties are broken by having each team bat for a one-over innings known as a Super Over; subsequent Super Overs may be played if the first Super Over ends in a tie. If this kind of match is temporarily interrupted by bad weather, then a complex mathematical formula, known as the Duckworth–Lewis–Stern method after its developers, is often used to recalculate a new target score. A one-day match can also be declared a "no-result" if fewer than a previously agreed number of overs have been bowled by either team, in circumstances that make normal resumption of play impossible; for example, wet weather.

In all forms of cricket, the umpires can abandon the match if bad light or rain makes it impossible to continue. There have been instances of entire matches, even Test matches scheduled to be played over five days, being lost to bad weather without a ball being bowled: for example, the third Test of the 1970/71 series in Australia.

- Innings

The innings (ending with 's' in both singular and plural form) is the term used for each phase of play during a match. Depending on the type of match being played, each team has either one or two innings. Sometimes all eleven members of the batting side take a turn to bat but, for various reasons, an innings can end before they have all done so. The innings terminates if the batting team is "all out", a term defined by the Laws: "at the fall of a wicket or the retirement of a batter, further balls remain to be bowled but no further batter is available to come in". In this situation, one of the batters has not been dismissed and is termed not out; this is because he has no partners left and there must always be two active batters while the innings is in progress.

- An innings may end early while there are still two not out batters

the batting team's captain may declare the innings closed even though some of his players have not had a turn to bat: this is a tactical decision by the captain, usually because he believes his team have scored sufficient runs and need time to dismiss the opposition in their innings

the set number of overs (i.e., in a limited overs match) have been bowled

the match has ended prematurely due to bad weather or running out of time

in the final innings of the match, the batting side has reached its target and won the game.

- Overs

The Laws state that, throughout an innings, "the ball shall be bowled from each end alternately in overs of 6 balls". The name "over" came about because the umpire calls "Over!" when six balls have been bowled. At this point, another bowler is deployed at the other end, and the fielding side changes ends while the batters do not. A bowler cannot bowl two successive overs, although a bowler can (and usually does) bowl alternate overs, from the same end, for several overs which are termed a "spell". The batters do not change ends at the end of the over, and so the one who was non-striker is now the striker and vice versa. The umpires also change positions so that the one who was at "square leg" now stands behind the wicket at the non-striker's end and vice versa.

- Clothing and equipment

English cricketer W. G. Grace "taking guard" in 1883. His pads and bat are very similar to those used today. The gloves have evolved somewhat. Many modern players use more defensive equipment than were available to Grace, most notably helmets and arm guards.

The wicket-keeper (a specialised fielder behind the batter) and the batters wear protective gear because of the hardness of the ball, which can be delivered at speeds of more than 145 kilometres per hour (90 mph) and presents a major health and safety concern.

Protective clothing includes pads (designed to protect the knees and shins), batting gloves or wicket-keeper's gloves for the hands, a safety helmet for the head and a box for male players inside the trousers (to protect the crotch area). Some batters wear additional padding inside their shirts and trousers such as thigh pads, arm pads, rib protectors and shoulder pads. The only fielders allowed to wear protective gear are those in positions very close to the batter (i.e., if they are alongside or in front of him), but they cannot wear gloves or external leg guards.

Subject to certain variations, on-field clothing generally includes a collared shirt with short or long sleeves; long trousers; woolen pullover (if needed); cricket cap (for fielding) or a safety helmet; and spiked shoes or boots to increase traction. The kit is traditionally all white and this remains the case in Test and first-class cricket but, in limited overs cricket, team colours are worn instead.

- Bat and ball

Two types of cricket ball, both of the same size:

i) A used white ball. White balls are mainly used in limited overs cricket, especially in matches played at night, under floodlights (left).

ii) A used red ball. Red balls are used in Test cricket, first-class cricket and some other forms of cricket (right).

The essence of the sport is that a bowler delivers (i.e., bowls) the ball from his or her end of the pitch towards the batter who, armed with a bat, is "on strike" at the other end (see next sub-section: Basic gameplay).

The bat is made of wood, usually Salix alba (white willow), and has the shape of a blade topped by a cylindrical handle. The blade must not be more than 4.25 inches (10.8 cm) wide and the total length of the bat not more than 38 inches (97 cm). There is no standard for the weight, which is usually between 2 lb 7 oz and 3 lb (1.1 and 1.4 kg).

The ball is a hard leather-seamed spheroid, with a circumference of 9 inches (23 cm). The ball has a "seam": six rows of stitches attaching the leather shell of the ball to the string and cork interior. The seam on a new ball is prominent and helps the bowler propel it in a less predictable manner. During matches, the quality of the ball deteriorates to a point where it is no longer usable; during the course of this deterioration, its behaviour in flight will change and can influence the outcome of the match. Players will, therefore, attempt to modify the ball's behaviour by modifying its physical properties. Polishing the ball and wetting it with sweat or saliva is legal, even when the polishing is deliberately done on one side only to increase the ball's swing through the air, but the acts of rubbing other substances into the ball, scratching the surface or picking at the seam are illegal ball tampering.

• Player roles

Basic gameplay: bowler to batter
During normal play, thirteen players and two umpires are on the field. Two of the players are batters and the rest are all eleven members of the fielding team. The other nine players in the batting team are off the field in the pavilion. The image with overlay below shows what is happening when a ball is being bowled and which of the personnel are on or close to the pitch.

• Return crease

In the photo, the two batters (3 & 8; wearing yellow) have taken position at each end of the pitch (6). Three members of the fielding team (4, 10 & 11; wearing dark blue) are in shot. One of the two umpires (1; wearing white hat) is stationed behind the wicket (2) at the bowler's (4) end of the pitch. The bowler (4) is bowling the ball (5) from his end of the pitch to the batter at the other end who is called the "striker". The other batter (3) at the bowling end is called the "non-striker". The wicket-keeper (10), who is a specialist, is positioned behind the striker's wicket (9) and behind him stands one of the fielders in a position called "first slip" (11). While the bowler and the first slip are wearing conventional kit only, the two batters and the wicket-keeper are wearing protective gear including safety helmets, padded gloves and leg guards (pads).

While the umpire (1) in shot stands at the bowler's end of the pitch, his colleague stands in the outfield, usually in or near the fielding position called "square leg", so that he is in line with the popping crease (7) at the striker's end of the pitch. The bowling crease (not numbered) is the one on which the wicket is located between the return creases (12). The bowler (4) intends to hit the wicket (9) with the ball (5) or, at least, to prevent the striker (8) from scoring runs. The striker (8) intends, by using his bat, to defend his wicket and, if possible, to hit the ball away from the pitch in order to score runs.

Some players are skilled in both batting and bowling, or as either or these as well as wicket-keeping, so are termed all-rounders. Bowlers are classified according to their style, generally as fast bowlers, seam bowlers or spinners. Batters are classified according to whether they are right-handed or left-handed.

• Fielding

Of the eleven fielders, three are in shot in the image above. The other eight are elsewhere on the field, their positions determined on a tactical basis by the captain or the bowler. Fielders often change position between deliveries, again as directed by the captain or bowler.

If a fielder is injured or becomes ill during a match, a substitute is allowed to field instead of him, but the substitute cannot bowl or act as a captain, except in the case of concussion substitutes in international cricket. The substitute leaves the field when the injured player is fit to return. The Laws of Cricket were updated in 2017 to allow substitutes to act as wicket-keepers.

- Bowling and dismissal

Glenn McGrath of Australia holds the world record for most wickets in the Cricket World Cup.

Most bowlers are considered specialists in that they are selected for the team because of their skill as a bowler, although some are all-rounders and even specialist batters bowl occasionally. The specialists bowl several times during an innings but may not bowl two overs consecutively. If the captain wants a bowler to "change ends", another bowler must temporarily fill in so that the change is not immediate.

A bowler reaches his delivery stride by means of a "run-up" and an over is deemed to have begun when the bowler starts his run-up for the first delivery of that over, the ball then being "in play".

Fast bowlers, needing momentum, take a lengthy run up while bowlers with a slow delivery take no more than a couple of steps before bowling. The fastest bowlers can deliver the ball at a speed of over 145 kilometres per hour (90 mph) and they sometimes rely on sheer speed to try to defeat the batter, who is forced to react very quickly.

Other fast bowlers rely on a mixture of speed and guile by making the ball seam or swing (i.e. curve) in flight. This type of delivery can deceive a batter into miscuing his shot, for example, so that the ball just touches the edge of the bat and can then be "caught behind" by the wicket-keeper or a slip fielder. At the other end of the bowling scale is the spin bowler who bowls at a relatively slow pace and relies entirely on guile to deceive the batter. A spinner will often "buy his wicket" by "tossing one up" (in a slower, steeper parabolic path) to lure the batter into making a poor shot. The batter has to be very wary of such deliveries as they are often "flighted" or spun so that the ball will not behave quite as he expects and he could be "trapped" into getting himself out. In between the pacemen and the spinners are the medium paced seamers who rely on persistent accuracy to try to contain the rate of scoring and wear down the batter's concentration.

There are nine ways in which a batter can be dismissed: five relatively common and four extremely rare. The common forms of dismissal are bowled, caught, leg before wicket (lbw), run out and stumped. Rare methods are hit wicket,hit the ball twice, obstructing the field and timed out. The Laws state that the fielding team, usually the bowler in practice, must appeal for a dismissal before the umpire can give his decision. If the batter is out, the umpire raises a forefinger and says "Out!"; otherwise, he will shake his head and say "Not out".There is, effectively, a tenth method of dismissal, retired out, which is not an on-field dismissal as such but rather a retrospective one for which no fielder is credited.

- Batting, runs and extras

The directions in which a right-handed batter, facing down the page, intends to send the ball when playing various cricketing shots. The diagram for a left-handed batter is a mirror image of this one.

Batters take turns to bat via a batting order which is decided beforehand by the team captain and presented to the umpires, though the order remains flexible when the captain officially nominates the team. Substitute batters are generally not allowed, except in the case of concussion substitutes in international cricket.

In order to begin batting the batter first adopts a batting stance. Standardly, this involves adopting a slight crouch with the feet pointing across the front of the wicket, looking in the direction of the bowler, and holding the bat so it passes over the feet and so its tip can rest on the ground near to the toes of the back foot.

A skilled batter can use a wide array of "shots" or "strokes" in both defensive and attacking mode. The idea is to hit the ball to the best effect with the flat surface of the bat's blade. If the ball touches the side of the bat it is called an "edge". The batter does not have to play a shot and can allow the ball to go through to the wicketkeeper. Equally, he does not have to attempt a run when he hits the ball with his bat. Batters do not always seek to hit the ball as hard as possible, and a good player can score runs just by making a deft stroke with a turn of the wrists or by simply "blocking" the ball but directing it away from fielders so that he has time to take a run. A wide variety of shots are played, the batter's repertoire including strokes named according to the style of swing and the direction aimed: e.g., "cut", "drive", "hook", "pull".

The batter on strike (i.e. the "striker") must prevent the ball hitting the wicket, and try to score runs by hitting the ball with his bat so that he and his partner have time to run from one end of the pitch to the other before the fielding side can return the ball. To register a run, both runners must touch the ground behind the popping crease with either their bats or their bodies (the batters carry their bats as they run). Each completed run increments the score of both the team and the striker.

- Sachin Tendulkar is the only player to have scored one hundred international centuries

The decision to attempt a run is ideally made by the batter who has the better view of the ball's progress, and this is communicated by calling: usually "yes", "no" or "wait". More than one run can be scored from a single hit: hits worth one to three runs are common, but the size of the field is such that it is usually difficult to run four or more. To compensate for this, hits that reach the boundary of the field are automatically awarded four runs if the ball touches the ground en route to the boundary or six runs if the ball clears the boundary without touching the ground within the boundary. In these cases the batters do not need to run. Hits for five are unusual and generally rely on the help of "overthrows" by a fielder returning the ball. If an odd number of runs is scored by the striker, the two batters have changed ends, and the one who was non-striker is now the striker. Only the striker can score individual runs, but all runs are added to the team's total.

Additional runs can be gained by the batting team as extras (called "sundries" in Australia) due to errors made by the fielding side. This is achieved in four ways: no-ball, a penalty of one extra conceded by the bowler if he breaks the rules; wide, a penalty of one extra conceded by the bowler if he bowls so that the ball is out of the batter's reach bye, an extra awarded if the batter misses the ball and it goes past the wicket-keeper and gives the batters time to run in the conventional way leg bye, as for a bye except that the ball has hit the batter's body, though not his bat. If the bowler has conceded a no-ball or a wide, his team incurs an additional penalty because that ball (i.e., delivery) has to be bowled again and hence the batting side has the opportunity to score more runs from this extra ball.

• Specialist roles

Captain (cricket) and Wicket-keeper
The captain is often the most experienced player in the team, certainly the most tactically astute, and can possess any of the main skillsets as a batter, a bowler or a wicket-keeper. Within the Laws, the captain has certain responsibilities in terms of nominating his players to the umpires before the match and ensuring that his players conduct themselves "within the spirit and traditions of the game as well as within the Laws".

The wicket-keeper (sometimes called simply the "keeper") is a specialist fielder subject to various rules within the Laws about his equipment and demeanour. He is the only member of the fielding side who can effect a stumping and is the only one permitted to wear gloves and external leg guards. Depending on their primary skills, the other ten players in the team tend to be classified as specialist batters or specialist bowlers. Generally, a team will include five or six specialist batters and four or five specialist bowlers, plus the wicket-keeper.

• Umpires and scorers

Umpire (cricket), Scoring (cricket), and Cricket statistics
An umpire signals a decision to the scorers

The game on the field is regulated by the two umpires, one of whom stands behind the wicket at the bowler's end, the other in a position called "square leg" which is about 15–20 metres away from the batter on strike and in line with the popping crease on which he is taking guard. The umpires have several responsibilities including adjudication on whether a ball has been correctly bowled (i.e., not a no-ball or a wide); when a run is scored; whether a batter is out (the fielding side must first appeal to the umpire, usually with the phrase "How's that?" or "Owzat?"); when intervals start and end; and the suitability of the pitch, field and weather for playing the game. The umpires are authorised to interrupt or even abandon a match due to circumstances likely to endanger the players, such as a damp pitch or deterioration of the light.

Off the field in televised matches, there is usually a third umpire who can make decisions on certain incidents with the aid of video evidence. The third umpire is mandatory under the playing conditions for Test and Limited Overs International matches played between two ICC full member countries. These matches also have a match referee whose job is to ensure that play is within the Laws and the spirit of the game.

The match details, including runs and dismissals, are recorded by two official scorers, one representing each team. The scorers are directed by the hand signals of an umpire . For example, the umpire raises a forefinger to signal that the batter is out (has been dismissed); he raises both arms above his head if the batter has hit the ball for six runs. The scorers are required by the Laws to record all runs scored, wickets taken and overs bowled; in practice, they also note significant amounts of additional data relating to the game.

A match's statistics are summarised on a scorecard. Prior to the popularisation of scorecards, most scoring was done by men sitting on vantage points cuttings notches on tally sticks and runs were originally called notches.According to Rowland Bowen, the earliest known scorecard templates were introduced in 1776 by T. Pratt of Sevenoaks and soon came into general use.It is believed that scorecards were printed and sold at Lord's for the first time in 1846.

- thank you for buy & read this book

    have a great day of your
    from : Mr Vivek Kumar Pandey

CPSIA information can be obtained
at www.ICGtesting.com
Printed in the USA
BVHW031408151122
651893BV00035B/662